EARTH WORDS

THE HUGH MacLENNAN POETRY SERIES
Editors: Allan Hepburn and Carolyn Smart

TITLES IN THE SERIES

Earth Words

Conversing with Three Sages

JOHN REIBETANZ

McGill-Queen's University Press
Montreal & Kingston • London • Chicago

ISBN 978-0-2280-0901-6 (paper)
ISBN 978-0-2280-1009-8 (ePDF)
ISBN 978-0-2280-1010-4 (ePUB)

Legal deposit fourth quarter 2021
Bibliothèque nationale du Québec

Printed in Canada on acid-free paper that is 100% ancient forest free
(100% post-consumer recycled), processed chlorine free

Funded by the   Financé par le
Government   gouvernement
of Canada   du Canada

Canada Council   Conseil des arts
for the Arts   du Canada

We acknowledge the support of the Canada Council for the Arts.

Nous remercions le Conseil des arts du Canada de son soutien.

Library and Archives Canada Cataloguing in Publication

Title: Earth words: conversing with three sages / John Reibetanz.

Names: Reibetanz, John, 1944– author.

Series: Hugh MacLennan poetry series.

Description: Series statement: The Hugh MacLennan poetry series

Identifiers: Canadiana (print) 20210238518 | Canadiana (ebook)
20210238534 | ISBN 9780228009016 (softcover) |
ISBN 9780228010098 (PDF) | ISBN 9780228010104 (EPUB)

Subjects: LCGFT: Poetry.

Classification: LCC PS8585.E448 E27 2021 | DDC C811/.54—dc23

This book was typeset by Marquis Interscript in 9.5/13 Sabon.

*In loving memory of J.M.R.
and our long conversation*

Selves are ephemeral aggregations, made of the enduring substances of life – connections and conversations.
David G. Haskell, *Songs of the Trees*

CONTENTS

EARTH WORDS

Talking with Wang An-shih

Wang An-shih (1021–1086), a Chinese artist-intellectual devoted to public service but never interested in power or its trappings, rose to become the Emperor's most trusted adviser and introduced sweeping social and political reforms that included open education, a merit-based civil service, and subsidies for poor farmers. He retired at age fifty-five to a simple rural life, writing commentaries on Buddhist sutras along with some of the finest poetry of the Song era. In his retirement, the conservatives came to power, dismantled his reforms, and defamed his reputation – a familiar story in our age. These glosas engage in a series of conversations with Wang An-shih's voice as found in the four-line stanzas at which he excelled.

A CALLING

In vast mountain silences, summit clouds tumble over one another,
and on the river, fluttering sand-ducks drift and dive as they like.

Delighting in this, all thought of return forgotten, I grow patient,
a guest facing west wind to study the distances of its chant beyond.

"Steady-Shield Monastery"   Wang An-shih

I've been searching for you, teacher, in the wrong place,
as if the narrow spine – your poems' backbone –
would take on flesh and voice, leap from its bookcase
and speak to me over the winter-wind monotone
howling among this city's vertical islands
and turning rain's glass curtains white as your hair.
Let me instead call you out of that west wind
which has carried your voice from Chiang-ning mountain
    passes
through the Pacific Cordillera's southern
mountains: vast silences, summit clouds tumbling over one
    another

to interweave your breath with misty exhalations
from granite throats, oneness of self and not-self
you practised on your ridgeline walks – slow, patient
dissolving of footfalls into the hills' recesses.
Let me return with you, riding an updraft
to where the sky's blue swell breaks on cloud-peaks,
then set me gently under thatched porch rafters
crisscrossed by swallows and chevroned with the flashing
of their orange wings. There, willows graze your paddock
and on the river, fluttering sand-ducks drift and dive as
    they like.

You'd spread a straw mat in wildflowering grasses.
As it unrolled I'd watch your hands, gripping the edges,
shade into mine, a oneness in two persons:
not sharing breath like throat singers' duets,
but taking the world in through one pair of pupils
that trace their ancestry back through generations
of orb-formation to the same primal blizzard
of stellar dust, and that share the same passion
for tracing on paper the calligraphy of nature.
Delighting in this, all thought of return forgotten, I grow
    patient

with the shifting snowscript on my window ledge,
both for the pictograph each flake contains
and only holds up to microscopic lenses
(a modesty in harmony with your Ch'an
teachings), and for snow's pristine overwriting
of the city's smudged asphalt and concrete lines.
We are snow in our fluttering drifting and diving;
and like you, listening for monastery bells
on the way to Chiang-ning, I cup an ear to the window,
earth's guest, facing west wind to study the distances of its
    chant beyond.

TRANSPORT

I gaze into moss at my brushwood gate, rainwater radiant,
then wander through spring, blossoms crowding branches

everywhere. People travel distant roads and never arrive,
but all day here, birds in song leave and come back again

"A Spring Day"   Wang An-shih

Some trudge in lines from bombed-out shells of tenements,
some scuttle crabwise under barbed fencing.
They hug whatever's most precious as they flee:
the woman her blanketed newborn, the boy a teddy
in Hogwarts T-shirt, the man a cased-up mandolin.
No matter how deeply their red eyes burn into me, I can't
reach out to grief trapped in a black rectangular screen
that transports it thousands of miles instantly,
and my eyes would rather be where, a thousand years
    distant,
you gazed into moss at your brushwood gate, rainwater
    radiant,

your own removal willed rather than forced,
the empire's collapse a future nightmare, not
rubble about your feet. Oh, to transport
the actual precious selves from their ruined present
to your protected arbour, safe in the past,
trading blackened pine skeletons and scorched,
cracked earth for gravelled, plum-umbrella'd footpaths,
happily lost in high seas of barley at harvest
or, later in autumn, gathering baskets of beechnuts,
or wandering through spring, blossoms crowding branches

with feathery dancing, far from orange-jacketed
fledglings crammed into shuddering rubber dinghies.
Like birds – or diviners – did you probe gullied backroads
for sources of hope, and come upon its wellsprings
not under earth but on it, in the steady outflow
of blossom to fruit, the effusion of green leaves,
and annual waves of song from the orioles?
There is no change of season in the black
rectangle, no height or depth but a levelled
everywhere. People travel distant roads and never arrive,

and moss, that offspring of water and rooted years,
can't gain a foothold on dust and twisted rebar.
Their home has slipped away into myth, like Hogwarts
or your Peachblossom Land at the end of an endless river,
and once all hope of going back is gone,
the road holds nothing more than going on.
What would they give – blanket in tatters,
miniature wand missing from teddy's fist,
music locked in a coffined mandolin –
for one day where birds in song leave and come back
   again?

I doze, a guest among topsy-turvy books,
then sit amid insect song. Isolate silence,

remnant lamp casting halos of darkness,
heavy dew settling across cold branches.

"Autumn Night"   Wang An-shih

The leaves of paper, butterfly-wing thin,
let light stream through, only one side of each
printed. The illustrations' hand-painted swatches
of colour, like a butterfly's wing-scales, sing
their blues and reds into your room's night
where, placed on pasteboard edges, their backs up,
dozens of other books with butterfly binding
(leaves folded, prayer-like) catch quick naps
between flights. Like them, head resting on desk,
you doze, a guest among topsy-turvy books,

inked shapes fluttering before your eyelids' screen.
After fleet aphorisms from Confucius
and the *Book of Changes'* ten-winged divinations,
Chunyu Fen, fresh from *his* fabled dream,
sweeps across yours: yellow-silk-robed and regal,
without stirring from his couch he's danced
through thirty imagined years; now, in the sequel,
no longer lulled by the court musician's guqin,
he awakens to subjects shrunk to gnats and flies
and sits amid insect song. Isolated, in silence,

you too open your eyes and wonder which
were the dream flights: those conjured up by black on
white pages, or those once flesh and blood, whisked off
by time? Or are day and night both spells of witchcraft?
Did Chuang Tzu dream he was a butterfly,
or was he dreamt by one? And life has passed
in a wink to metamorphose Wang An-shih
into *The Old Man of the East City*,
whose freshly emergent radiant spark is now
a remnant lamp casting halos of darkness.

Half robed in self-pity's flowing gown,
you catch yourself in a version of Wang Tu's
ancient mirror, the deep reflecting pool
that dispels evil spirits. Your rainbowed
fan-tail blazons you less butterfly
than peacock, privileged garden-strutting creature
brought indoors for the winter. You could not survive
among real tortoiseshells rather than paper ones,
sleeping for warmth in tree holes, hunched as
heavy dew settles across cold branches.

Gathering and keeping is an arrogant greed.
Heaven's loom of origins works its own way.

       ...

How can river and lake be inside these eyes?
Last night I dreamed wild billows and swells.

"Autumn Wind"   Wang An-shih

Once upon a time, there lives a king
      who loves gold as much as lying.
He orders plaster walls and wooden doors
      plated in gold; on palace floors
twenty-four carat frozen rivers thread
      through marble fields; thickly spread
on inconvenient truths, lies glitter from
      page and screen. No troublesome
bird in his kingdom is allowed to tweet
      that gathering and keeping is an arrogant greed.

The only gold to beguile you, ancient one,
      is drawn from plum trees by spring sun
and tarnishes to green – which you accept,
      knowing no riches may be kept.
The orders that blossom and fruit must obey
      are those of birth, growth, and decay.
Matter, awakening to glimpse the infinite,
      falls back into earth's dream of it
as day shuttles into night, night into day,
      Heaven's loom of origins working its own way.

More mythical than he dreams in his gold-clad
        tower, the king pursues godhead,
his hair the colour of the juice he sips
        from gilt-rimmed crystal so his lips
touch nothing that will rust. His frescoed skies
        stop the celestial clock at sunrise,
floating immortal with his groundless lies.
        Gold brows, in portraits that surround
his throne, arch over interstellar ice:
        how can river and lake be inside those eyes?

Many times upon a time, the dragon
        wakes in waters near your garden
snarling, its spiked tail flailing the waves to froth,
        its white teeth tearing at the shore
to mock the claims of land it sends cascading
        as if stone walls were sandcastles.
It renders crystal goblets down to beach glass
        and chews frescoes into flotsam.
After news reports of the latest scandals
        last night, I dreamed wild billows and swells.

I rollick through wildflower grasses,
sit alone on reed-crush cushions all

thatch-hut quiet. Old sun, treasured
guest, is it this good where you live?

"I rollick"   Wang An-shih

Letters come every day from the capital
        like giant snowflakes falling
on your doorstep, heralding the winter
        of your lifework's undoing:
the "new brooms" with no straw – all your reforms
        deformed by the crassest
self-servers – the poor flattered and then ignored,
        the writings of wise scholars
trashed. Yet still, unshaken by these losses,
        you rollick through wildflower grasses

        as if the willow's yellow
will brighten into gold epaulettes of spring
        instead of tarnishing
to a bronzed age, or as if your eyes opened
        a sluicegate in thick cloud
for sun to pour through. Even in the chill
        of first light, sandal-clad,
you gathered the orchard's last plums, and now
        for your mid-day meal you'll
sit alone on crushed reeds – cushions all

too cushy – and nibble the tart fruit, pocketing
        the tapered almond centres
for planting, so their sickle-sided Absence
        will once more glow with Presence,
as life transforms its Lasts into its Firsts.
        Feeling your spirit closer
to the hub of nature's great wheel when birdsong
        mingles with brush-stroke,
you work all afternoon in the garden, your
        thatch hut quiet. Old sun-treasured

        teacher, minding your view
that, as the tree has never owned its fruit,
        the yield of human hand
or voice is a mere breath to be surrendered
        to the surrounding air
which folds it back into regenerative
        readiness, I see your
Garden more a flowering pattern of thought
        than sheltered place, and I've
guessed it is this Good where you live.

Following thoughts all brush-bramble my hands open through,
I trace ridgelines, cross creeks, climb out onto terraces beyond:

the simplest wind-and-dew bridge, a little-boat moon cast adrift,
and birds widowed or lost, their comings and goings at an end.

"Following thoughts"   Wang An-shih

I hear it over a thousand-year distance,
and because music threads ear's labyrinth,
riding on air into the slot canyons
of the brain – not stopping at glass gates to linger
as a voyeur – it overpowers shadows
thrown on the eye's back wall from mute adieus
waved by our century's departed choruses
of extinct singers: pipers, warblers, snipes,
doves and curlews unheard now. To a mind bruised
following thoughts all brush-bramble, your hands open –
    through

the guqin's seashell-tipped frets – avenues
to a full-winged world. The five silk strings that vibrate
with creation's raw materials – earth,
fire, water, wood, and metal – learned
their signature songs from leafed, furred, or feathered
wind instruments of nature, plucked silk tuned
to the free rhythms of river-and-mountain weather.
Winging me into your landscape, every struck note
now gives rise to fresh ground: guided by your hand
I trace ridgelines, cross creeks, climb out onto terraces
    beyond

the lands and waters of my own place and time.
When fingered, the *hui* seashell spots sing back
the murmur of Pearl River current on sand, once captured
by the shell's ear, and your wutong soundboard hums
with generations of bees that thronged its blossoms –
all out-of-doors your voicing room, a loft
that also gave voice to the unmapped cosmos
within ourselves. At a loss for its name,
hand-holding lovers speak their own precarious uplift in
the simplest wind-and-dew bridge; a little-boat moon cast
  adrift

tells their old loneliness, as a squirrel's tail
trembles their skittishness. Our perseverance
echoes through swamp forests as the ivory-billed
woodpecker knocks twice, and twice again
in search of food – but only for as long as
forest and bird endure. What indigo-sequined
cape will pride don when the last peacock's call
has faded? Without the owl, who sees who's wise?
Without the gulls' cries, will we shed silent tears for friends
and birds widowed or lost, their comings and goings at an
  end?

History-mist and cloud-blur, waters boundless and beyond,
weed-tangled city walls wrap around ruins. Brush-choked

sight's a lifetime of world-dust lamenting all our struggles,
the past traced everywhere in thought, impossible to forget.

"Thinking of Golden-Tomb City Long Ago" Wang An-shih

            Ruins were nothing new
         even a thousand years ago
when you would steal beyond the pantiled walls
         of the Chiang-ning you knew
      to play among half-buried bones
of the old city – stumps of columns standing
            guard over doorless doorsills
         where ghosts left footsteps in the dew
on mornings when your gaze and river-haze twinned
history-mist and cloud-blur, waters boundless; and beyond

            a jagged fragment of arch,
         the daily rounds of the long-dead
lived, as if one same ribbon of silk unscrolled
            the rainbow-making reach
         of your make-believing childhood
with earth's green unfolding. Bamboo shoots poked
            through dry stone troughs and spilled
         cascades of leaves your wishful heart
changed to flowing robes. Desire likened
weed-tangled city walls wrapped around ruins to basking

dragons coiled half-hidden
under waves of grass – fires banked,
but leaf scales flickering in light spring winds.
Looked at from a distance
and between your fingers, sunken
beams became rising ones, the peaks and gables
of a child-high skyline
free of old towers' long shadows,
the swords and fires that toppled them, their rubbled
sites a lifetime of world-dust lamenting all the struggles

of the past. And after
all things made here have been unmade –
the stone walls picked apart down to the last
nubbed chunk of rice-mortar –
that old city of your playtime,
peopled by your imagination yet
stands firm, roots anchored fast
in memory's rich subsoil where
like a dragon vine it ramifies, its fruit
your past traced everywhere in thought, impossible to forget.

RUINS 2

You would have known and loved
the place four hundred years before,
when the whale-nosed sea ran up the Narrows
as up the Pearl River
seeding with salt the reed beds where
oysters took root. Before the soon-depleted
soil was cropped with tobacco,
before rainfalls nursed the waves
with sewage, long before the child-me met
a past traced everywhere in thought, impossible to forget

when its decay stole up
my nose with every breath of pure
Gowanus. Tincture of coal tar, sulphur, chain oil,
floating furred corpses,
feces, conspired to kill the water.
On still days, it staged its own funeral:
the black-ooze-lined canal,
the slow flow. Ruined palaces
that you once played among flickered with clear
water reflecting trees kingfisher-green and vines silvered
azure,

but here the tenements
of green and blue fell into ruin –
wild meadows levelled, their resident nestlings
evicted, brooks and trout
ditched in the dust, sunfish eclipsed
forever when their pond succumbed to pavement.
When the last of Chiang-ning's
blues and greens have greyed to concrete,
how long will even your mountain-nestled,
sublime monasteries survive? People say "but I'm content

to visit nature in
parks and preserves," as if nature
were some distant cousin rather than
our body's second skin.
After an old disaster, your
ancestor Du Fu wrote, "The state's in ruins,
but rivers and mountains
persist." Yet, once that mesh of vein
and flesh unravels, there's no hope in hoping
to sail ravaged canals back into the inner pattern of things.

ANCHORAGE

It's all mirage illusion, like cinnabar-and-azure paintings, this
human world. We wander here for a time, then vanish into dust.

Things aren't other than they are. That's all anyone can know.
Don't ask if this thing I am today is the thing I was long ago.

"Self-Portrait"   Wang An-shih

You anchor your little boat midstream, moonlight
a spill of silver change over the waves.
Unlike Li Po, you won't be tempted to scoop it
up and dive into a flowing grave,
nor – never one to cosy up to mirrors –
will you drown in love with your own visage.
Adept of nature-prints, you've scanned the river's
gallery and come upon this vista
of moon and mountain others might dismiss
as mirrored illusion. Yet, like cinnabar-and-azure paintings,
    this

watercolour's source is earth and sky,
and unlike their art, it's a *motion* picture
thanks to the current – drifter, card shark
compulsively shuffling its pack of reflections.
We find our portraits in the picture cards,
both out-of-date: you, robed in pre-fustian
silks gleaming like sun on a rock face,
me with long hair willowing to the shoulder,
filmy avatars of a seeming-robust
human world. We wander here for a time, then vanish into
    mist,

and the river you anchor in pours out the hours
of our changes, becomes – as if it coursed
through artery and vein rather than gorge –
logged in the body's esperanto, word
for *fleeting*. So our mouths devour the mountain
and speak it out for *lasting*, and moonglow
expresses *longing*, which the water's tongues
draw out still further. This world's things are the heart's
language primer, yet in your time and now
things as they are are Other, and all anyone can know

of them are signs we half-read through the stream's
ripples. Teacher of nature's lexicon,
you've hooked the anchor of your boat-classroom
into the flood itself – no objects fixed
and all verbs transitive: in earth's deep grammar,
Tai Mountain's as changeable as its heavenly echo,
the moon. As, now, this visit turns to your
guest-gifting me a free translation from
the elemental idiom of flow:
"Don't ask if this thing I am today is the thing I was long
   ago."

Overnight rain purifies royal parkland.
Morning sun exalts the imperial city.

In good years, all harvest joy, people
dance on gravemounds, music pulsing.

"Early Autumn"   Wang An-shih

Give or take a thousand years, he
could be you or me, napping on
a slat bench under this oak tree,
which might have graced your emperor's garden
(ranged around its pond-framed lotus, symbol
of purity) but instead sits on an island
mid-city: Queen's Park, asphalt-river-circled
backyard of Parliament. He dreams
windblown leaves into water. Sounds of
overnight rain purify royal parkland

of droppings (dog or pigeon), long
as eyes stay closed. They open on
no silk-robed ruler, but bronzed King
Edward astride his horse, whose outsized gen-
itals some wag has sprayed with Day-Glo, maybe
to symbolize the rider's alacrity
at stud. When, freed from Empire, Delhi
expelled this British horse and king,
the refugees landed here, where gritty
morning sun exalts no imperial city,

but welcomes tarnished émigrés
like them, him, you or me, under
the patched umbrella of this tree,
island on an island billowed round
with trucks' monoxide wakes, garden whose sundials
are the tilted shadows of flaking slate steeples
and the oak's zigzag branches, pock-leaved
but prolific. From strewn acorns
squirrelled away, scores of black squirrels
in good years will harvest joy; people

like this now-wakened napper will
find peace in the tree's gap-roofed room.
Shouldering the rucksack that pillowed
a whirling head after his morning midterm,
he fords the light-stopped rapids of traffic,
repeating without risk the island-hopping
that brought his parents to this mottled city
from ancient empires where killers
out of pure, unbridled impulse
danced on gravemounds, singing.

Remnant coffins will poke out how many springs from now,
and tangled weeds in desolate winds bury magic horses.

It isn't like long ago, gravemound guests drunk and well-fed:
now they come gathering sticks and dry grass for their fires.

"At Broken-Tomb Shores"   Wang An-shih

        Islanded, your dead ancestors
        (partnered with their gear, fisher
        pillowed by net, bow embraced
by hunter) anchored in cliffside coffins far
above spring floods that yearly roared and fell
silent, but this Atlantic island's gravemounds
and all they hold lie helpless under a spell
        of forever-rising waters.
        Washing away, row upon row,
remnant coffins will poke out not many springs from now,

        no match for foaming, stampeding herds
        of breakers that will pound the frail
        cargo to splinters, polished slate shards
blowing away like so many ceremonial
feathers, gone missing with the birds whose wings
surfed the deep-troughed waves of marram grass
that caressed the shoreline – red knots, bobolinks,
        piping plovers braiding the air
        where salt-bleached toppling wooden crosses
and weeds tangled by desolate winds are buried by the storm
  horses.

Lennox Island's Atlantic coast
seems as distant from Chiang-ning's
Stone Mountain as the earliest
Mi'kmaq campsite from the metal-pinnacled
ninety-storey tower that outsteeps
your mountain now; yet flats and talls are coupled
in loss, as if Pangaea were re-stitched
into one land of people cursed
with grieving numberless departed.
It isn't like long ago, gravemound guests drunk and well-fed:

no funeral service now, no party
of descendants. The deceased
have taken all their progeny
out of the world and into history,
finless porpoise bodiless, Yangtze dolphin
swimming past water, ladyslipper flowers
tiptoeing off the earth. Our own children
dispossessed from their steel towers
by this inverted evolution
will soon come gathering sticks and dry grass for their fires.

Alone, a noon dove calling in spring
shade, I lie in a valley of forest quiet.

Scraps of cloud pass, scattering rain,
and I listen, late in life, to its clatter.

"Thoughts as I Lie Alone" Wang An-shih

The drums wake you, your hut is under attack:
   clouds launch thousands of rain-arrows.
Some pierce the layered thatch, bright tips melting
   into puddles on your floor,
some rattle down the drawn bamboo shades
   or hit the porch deck, drenching
the sandals you've left out, now nobody's
   reminded you to bring them back
in. Cries go unheard. You're not used to being
   alone, a lone dove calling in spring

   for its fellow brooder. Funny
old bird, you've never been one to fly solo
   like the migrant goose Po Chü-i
set free, nor is your feathery white forelock
   rain-proof – "or even sun-proof," you
murmur, remembering how your mate,
   dove-like in her devotion, used
to scuttle after you with an umbrella
   for noontime walks. Now utter
shade, she lies in a valley of forest quiet.

Not walking tonight, though it roves above the rain,
          the moon rushes from cloud to cloud,
a plump white dove in flight. What sustains it
          in its solitude? Does it browse
among the tiny blossoms of the stars,
          or is it too consumed with pain
to give a thought to creature comforts? Its pallor,
          like what you face in your round mirror,
argues hunger, yet it endures. Thin
          scraps of cloud pass, scattering rain,

          but the moon holds up its mountains
in the inconstant sky, as it did when you
          and she, first holding hands, counted
the lamps spangling the wall of heaven's Supreme
          Palace. As it did before
you both were born, and as it will long after
          rain, driven wild by the glower
of the moon's marble eye, will have brought off
          this siege to scour your bones still whiter
while you listen, late in life, to its clatter.

I close my gate, wanting to end grief,
but grief won't go away. Then spring

wind comes, and I want to keep grief
close, but somehow grief won't stay.

"Just to Say"   Wang An-shih

Why haven't you become a monk
to wall out the world's miseries? You've gone
        halfway, leaving the riverbank's
cargoes of crying news, living among
        those mountain monasteries where
silence stands guard over saffron-robed belief
        and soul-clouds float through the clear air.
But the lippy, red-robed sprite at your core
        murmurs you'd find scant relief
closing your gate, wanting to end grief.

Even if fingers pivot the little gates
        of skin to block your ear canals,
the river in your veins carries a downbeat
        you share with all the world's mortals,
one that rouses an upbeat in response,
        from chest-percussive apes to clicking
crickets, a music that confronts onrush
        with sostenuto, as a nightingale
meets April days with twenty-four turns on its song.
        No, grief won't go for good. Yet, spring

colours the numbed branches with
flights and flourishes, the thrush's *wee're okay*
        twining with the down-to-earth
questionings of the mourning dove to make
        a counterpoint between them, each
note unfurling unburdened as a fresh leaf.
        "Spring brings the respite of shared speech,"
I say, "but in the absence of shared breath.
        What can voice do? When winter's stiff
wind comes, and I want to keep grief

from storming my solitude, who will teach me how?"
        You point to a tousled "o" of a bird
whose sober grey headfeathers could be the cowl
        of some woeful sect; but, stirred
to song, the Garden Warbler burbles forth
        ungated giggles, all breathless play –
lone avian Li Po, chasing grief with mirth
        that, like the wine stains on his beard,
steeps the chill air. Silence will come at day's
        close, but somehow grief won't stay.

DOUBLE EXPOSURE

Ravaged chrysanthemums blacken. Autumn wind returns,
and rain like the rain when early plums ripen to yellow.

Hand in hand, why talk? We gaze together into grief every-
where in sight. Isn't this where mind knows itself utterly?

"Parting in River-Serene"   Wang An-shih

The eye wants the hand to follow it out of time,
reach beyond the ever-leaving world
and grip this vase of eternity in bloom.
A hundred winters have not wilted its flowers,
sun-yellows and sky-blues never knowing night.
Yet the mirror behind them reflects only urn
and flowers, will not let us into its sights;
and beyond Cézanne's artfully controlled climate,
seasons rage on. Early snow bites, frostburn-
ravaged chrysanthemums blacken, autumn wind returns

our breath chilled. You know there's no such thing
as still life, and he knew it too, planting
the vase with paper flowers to arrest
their fall. Your favourite kind of art opens
a window onto life as motion: take
Dong Yuan's *Riverbank*, tracking the charged flow
from mountain cataract to wave-chiselled basin,
cane-braced peasants like bamboo stalks bowing
near to snapping as they do when windblown,
and rain like the rain when early plums ripen to yellow

before they go soft. Caught in midstream, taunted
by water's shifting vacancies, we both thirst
for the opaque liquors of ink or paint,
hoping their pigments will grip and hold traces
of life's own radical impasto – even as
rose madder bloom dims on a canvassed tree,
script fades, and lead white blackens cumulus
to stormcloud. Parted by the same ruinous currents,
though we can never walk through the debris
hand in hand, we talk. We gaze together into grief every-

where we look, but as we talk, we look
through grief and see the landscapes of each other's
living being – as, when we read a book,
we move beyond fixed characters into a further
orbit of meaning, the full human presence
reached by entering in, stormswept refugees
of Dong's shadowy hills finding essential
shelter in mountain clefts no brushstrokes
catch, saying *I see* although none can see
where by sight. Isn't this where mind itself sees utterly?

*I've travelled this land five times in seven years, and at last
laugh in wonder. It's such majesty to be alive in this world,*

*to become another bundle of dry grain stored up, a lone old
man somehow sharing the idleness of generations to come.*

"Visiting River-Serene"   Wang An-shih

How long a hike to six hundred years before
your time, and sixteen hundred before mine?
And all uphill, higher than blossomers'
roots can tap water, higher than white pines
find earth-pockets to grip. Xie Ling-yün's hut,
perched on cloud peaks above where stone effaced
itself, offered the sole repose of utter
emptiness, until Meng Haoran –
gone hiking three centuries closer in the past –
travelled this land five times in seven years, and at last

put down his staff, sat cross-legged, and waited
for the mountain of repose to bow to him.
Seasons unfurled like scrolls, light and shade sprouted
from dormant stillness, but the north face of the same
mountain frowned on his follower Du Fu:
earth heaved like a thawing river, winds hurled
him down and drove the clouds' furious tears through him,
the moon a tear in the eye of his starving child.
After his trials, what kind of traveller would
*laugh in wonder and think it such majesty to be alive in this
    world?*

Po Chü-I, whose own children the insatiable land
had swallowed one by one, never lost faith
in the star-matter at the heart of earth.
He journeyed deep into the near-at-hand,
scrubbing river pebbles to release
traces of ancient sky-gleam, folding back
the turf blanket to peek at future trees
asleep in seeds, consigning his digs' finds
to ink-flecked parchment rolled into a scroll
to become another bundle of dry grain stored up:
    place-holder

for later wayfarers like you, eating the grain
with your eyes, being transported by its taste
to a country where rivers and mountains
hold their inked shapes and those same shapes infused
with others' looking and listening, footsteps
and paddle-strokes in motion, journey's outcome
never the same for any two explorers
repairing to those banked tracks, yesterday's,
today's or tomorrow's lone woman or lone
man somehow sharing the inner trails of generations to
    come.

AUTUMN RIVERS

Across a thousand hundred-twist trails through forest hills,
a painting's wind-mist silvers autumn into a single colour,

nothing left but the beauty of wandering out impulse here.
Red poplar-tears: what grief scatters them across streams?

"Across a thousand"   Wang An-shih

Now comes the dwindling time, yet these roads, like
       your rivers, leap and coil, as if
           earth rode a flood tide welling
up from wind-roiled green seas of pine and oak,
       each trunk a time-carved pictograph
          evoking veined gorge walls
for you, for me these grooved networks of winding
       sideroads. You and I both seek
         a centre: here the way spills
across a thousand hundred-twist trails through forest hills

whose billowing green will soon be tinged with flames,
       as oak and poplar clothe themselves
         in red and yellow robes
of a sun setting early behind columns
       of Eastern white pine, sentinels
          doubled in dark lake mirrors.
Your way to the centre winds through fact and fable:
       from river fog – as from a dream –
         pine ghosts rise – or as where
a painting's wind-mist silvers autumn into a single colour,

the near more distinct, the distant more faint, until
             substance becomes mere counterpoise
                    for insubstantial, life
weaving the same pattern seen from front
             or back. My way meets yours when snows
                    make one gauze veil of shore
and iced lake – presence and absence sifting through
             each other, all impulse to contrast
                    our wanderings muted where
nothing's left but a beauty outwandering impulse. Here,

we both learn from the frogs how to keep green
             green under white ice. We practise
                    their slow breathing, leave off
croaking out the *like* or *as* that turns their scene
             into our scenario, accept
                    the *is* that seamlessly
weaves us into their meshwork, rivulets
             where leaf-thin skin breathes the air in
                    water, but no trees weep
red poplar-tears, no grief scatters leaves across streams.

HARMONIES

When a spirit-spring broke open, it began
swelling and coiling on ahead and through

mountains crowded up, blocking the way.
It keeps on flowing right on time to the sea.

"River"   Wang An-shih

Our legends get it wrong, keeping the clock
out of the garden of some golden age
(yours in Peachblossom Land, mine in God's Park),
so blush will never ripen into blaze.
How can you sink your teeth into pink petals,
and when, without a when, will earth's new tenants
be brought forth? Life's rife with unsettling changes
as substance turns to self and self turns back
to substance once again. In the beginning,
when a spirit-spring broke open, it began

by searching for a partner to share time's song,
day courting night outside, *lub* shacking up
with *dub* deep down, yin chasing after yang
in every corner. This creation opera
cast Echo as a necessary voice:
she is the dark side of Narcissus' moon,
without whom he would never find wholeness.
When they sing their duets, the spirit-spring
fountains up, note overflows note, their music
swelling and coiling on ahead and through

age upon age, like the dragon rising
after winter from your river's deeps.
Or like your voice, stilled under the black ice
of ink on parchment, waking from long sleep
to find itself stirring in a strange land –
not the thin-pinioned, quivering butterfly
of Chuang Tzu's vision or the deplumed commander
of Chunyu Fen's, but quick with song, enlightened,
sailing aloft, though centuries as high
as mountains crowded up, blocking the way.

Our voices in duet sailed in and out
of our contrails, each playing Echo to
the other. Every breath let go of bits
of what was once ourselves, and then took on
another set of castoffs. We became
two river vessels jettisoning dinghy,
wheelhouse, planking, who by calling them
back into being kept ourselves afloat,
making one song of what's you and what's me.
It keeps time, flowing right on to the sea.

Walking with Henry Thoreau

Henry David Thoreau (1817–1862) is known as the
author of *Walden*, yet that work constituted only a small
though vital part of a prodigious output, some of which
was published posthumously (*Cape Cod*, *The Maine
Woods*) and some of which remained unfinished at his
death (*Wild Fruits*, *The Dispersion of Seeds*). Most
recently, fuller attention has been given to the two-million
words of his *Journal*, now recognized as a work of art
in its own right and much more than a source for his
other writings. These glosas converse with a broad range
of Thoreau's writings. Although not chronologically
organized, this sequence attempts to reflect the
development of his thoughts and interests both before
and after *Walden*. Italicized words and phrases within
stanzas are direct quotations from Thoreau's writings,
with the exception of some quoted birdsong.

SCOPE

The shallowest still water
is unfathomable. Wherever
the trees and skies are reflected
there is more than Atlantic depth.

A Week on the Concord and Merrimack
Rivers ("Sunday")   Henry D. Thoreau

Beyond eye's reach, remote
from ear's tapped drum, new worlds
open down the narrow
corridors of micro
or telescope. The moon's
smooth, familiar features
crater with volcanoes
and crags, far brown furrows
sprout green hedgerows, and under
the shallowest still water

a domed city of alien
creatures bustles, one-eyed
serpents with spiked tails
lashing globules they ride
along shifting canals.
Yet every such scene, whether
in night sky's lit palace,
next-door neighbour's cornfield,
or drop spilled on your floor,
is unfathomable Wherever

when you're imprisoned in
the hollow tube whose glass
vistas seem less seen
than dreamt, a ghostly closeness
touch can never push
away, lying distanced
as something purely wished for –
like the river's shining
mirror, where interleafed
trees and skies are reflected

but cannot offer nest
to bird or cloud. Or you,
who never can find rest
except when striding through
full-bodied nearnesses
as fully embodied self
(not Emerson's "eyeball"); who senses
that in this world possessed
by muscle, skin, and breath,
there is more than Atlantic depth.

FIELD OF VISION

In distant woods or fields, I come to myself,
I once more feel myself grandly related ...
It is as if I had come to an open window ...
met in those places some grand ... immortal ... companion.

Journal, 7 January 1857   Henry D. Thoreau

I've been searching for you, teacher, in the wrong place:
a sliver-thin shimmer's simulated view –
the crystal palace that is all façade,
this window I look at but never through.
How will my eyes, trapped in their fixed focus
an arm's length away, see through the veil
of far-off lifetimes? How will your cabined voice
breach the cyberspace that holds my senses
anaesthetized, under a digital spell?
In distant woods or fields, I come to myself,

and come towards you, by waking to the world's
living connectivity, pupils
dilating or contracting as clouds furl
and unfurl under the same sun, nostrils
opening wide to catch the breath we share
with every other breather, whether rooted
and leafed or winged and climbing hills of air.
I hear the same trilled insistence in the whippoorwills,
the sleek brook purring to some stiller water,
and once more feel myself grandly related,

twinned with you in the mist that cools my forehead
when I step down from the barley field through tall
bluestems to a low track canopied
by pitch pines, my running shoes' rubber soles
squeaking out duets with nighthawks high
above the star-sheened branches. You would know
the joy of happening on the night sky
spread like a coverlet upon a bed
of lake. I would not need to tell you how
it is as if I had come to an open window

giving onto a field flowered with stars,
heaven's anemones blooming in the furrows
ploughed by the wind, a tracery far more
antique than any gothic cathedral's rose
and more divine because not entombed in stone
but quickened by the lake's pulse, alive with motion.
And when, in midnight calms, the smooth-skinned moon
that met your eyes meets mine among the mirrored
clouds and treetops, you and I, as one,
meet in those places some grand immortal companion.

THE HARP

To ears that are expanded what a harp this world is!
The occupied ear thinks that beyond the cricket
no sound can be heard – but there is an immortal melody
that may be heard ... by ears that can attend.

Journal, 21 July 1851   Henry D. Thoreau

You are attuned to Concord's music before
the Fitchburg Railroad anchors instruments
along the track through the Deep Cut, where their wires
trill when strumming fingers of wind caress
the wood-framed lines. You shiver at the shrill,
hawk-like peal of the locomotive's whistle
or the sharps of its wheels as they graze the curved rail
around the pond. If steam engines' bursts of pressure
at evening sound like nightingale-chanted vespers
to ears that are expanded, what a harp this world is

to you, each being plucking its singular string.
Before the pines are trimmed into telegraph poles
or squared into sleepers, you hear them transposing
the north wind's shuddering chords into needle-
quiver, while through their branches Heywood's brook
carries a light tune on the damp, thick air
of night. The course such music follows is like
no lines any citified composer
might chart: invaded by ticking clocks
the occupied ear thinks that beneath the cricket's

chirp, a hard-shelled metronome counts off
measures of time, but the cricket sings from beyond,
plucking an angel's harp, *unaffected*
by sun and moon. It is a midnight sound
heard at noon – a midday sound heard at midnight.
You witness an annunciation when apple trees
break into song, overwhelming your sight
with blossoms, rose-quintet flourishes
prefiguring fruit. As far as the eye can see
no sound can be heard – but there is an immortal melody

ringing the pink petals, as when yellow lichens
choir the bare north sides of wintering aspens
with anthems of summer sun, or the dry scent
of a corn tassel heralds coming ripeness –
descants of fragrance and colour borne on air
like sound waves. The most divine redolence
falls rather than rises from thin white wires
strung from the clouds, a harp whose concord
drifts the earth in whispers of transcendence
that may be heard by ears that can attend.

BATTERY FED

Fewer thoughts visit ... from year to year,
for the grove in our minds is laid waste ...
scarcely a twig left for them to perch on ...
Our winged thoughts are turned to poultry.

"Walking"   Henry D. Thoreau

Your heart consorts with birds. Whether
in wingbeat or songbeat, two are one:
morning rooster as your *feathered*
wakeful thought, owl-wails as un-
housed *human sobs* from the soul's *stark*
twilight woods. The plumage you wear
(clay-brown corduroy upperparts)
marks you as kin to Concord Forest's
wood thrush, whose call tickles your ear
though fewer visit from year to year,

brown camouflage not enough to shield them
from toxic rain among sparse trees.
Though we might just catch their morning hymns –
the soft notes of their *ee-oh-lays* –
or their alarmed machine-gun *pit-*
pit-pit, above the clanging haste
of the 8:05 through the Deep Cut,
we sit cut off from trill or din,
earbud and iPhone interlaced
while the grove in our minds is laid waste

by ant-high tyrants who broadcast
from glass-screened, hand-sized podiums.
They take eyes hostage, training them
on ciphered lines. Shapes from your past –
those free-wheeling, half-avian,
half-angelic figures – search
our inner and outer woods in vain.
Where the sky's callers used to nest
in dancing crowns of ash or birch
there's scarcely a twig for them to perch on.

Our train pauses. The window frames
a feathered body, also paused
and hunched like ours. It teeters from
a lip of bark on curled-up claws,
keels over like a heart victim,
then – scissor wingstrokes cutting free
from earth's plumb line – takes off as if
slingshot. The swift becomes its name
while, gifted with uncaged poetry,
our winged thoughts are turned to poultry.

The thought of some work ... will run in my head
and I am not where my body is ...
In my walks I would return
to my senses like a bird or a beast.

Journal, 28 November 1850   Henry D. Thoreau

Walk with me, Henry, and guide me
to hear and see: ears catching earth's broadcast
        beyond what you call *the almost*
incessant hum of your own personal factory,
        eyes like those of the woodchuck who,
though smaller than your shoe, stood ground and stared
        you down, wheeling around to front you
step by step, eyes sharp as its gritted teeth.
        When my mind should go where my feet lead,
the thought of some work will run through my head,

draw down the shades, and stop up the side vents,
        as if the moth you watched unfold
and spread unwrinkling ermined wings were pulled
        back into its cocoon. Winter
snow may epaulette my shoulders, weaving
        my hat a second brim, adding inches
to dry-stone walls I scale; spring pollen may leave
        yellow streaks on sleeves swept by
willow catkins, or may invade my nostrils,
        but I am not where my body is,

and seasons to me are marked by crossing out
        numbers on a grid, not crossing
timbers basked in sun or coated with frost
        above sprinting or sleeping water.
When early sunshine tempts me from my shell,
        if you come with me, I might learn
to listen for returning blackbirds *calling*
        the summer months along, their haste
clipping short their cries, so strong the yearning.
        In my walks I would return

        not only to known fields, but to
the grackle or the redwing at my core,
        thinking with every tautened feather
in touch with updraft, eddy, calm, and flow –
        like the flying squirrel you watched
spring from the top of a tall maple and coast
        through intertwined hemlock branches
without grazing a twig – in balance mo-
        ment by moment, unboxed, released
to my senses like a bird or a beast.

COMBATANTS

Meanwhile the earth jogged steadily on
In her mantle of purest white,
And anon another spring was born
When winter was vanished quite

"The Bluebirds"   Henry D. Thoreau

If *they are all beasts*
of burden, carrying a share
of *our thoughts,* as you say, then even the least
muscled of them must bear
some weighty notion. You witnessed ants
turn wood chips into hills and trenches strewn
with wounded combatants,
severed antennae, plated breasts
torn open, dead fangs clamped on carrion.
Meanwhile the earth jogged steadily on,

shadows ploughed casualties
into the dark and, having outfought
two red foes, the giant black ant you studied
ditched their heads and limped off.
Your *harrowed* thoughts recall my own
at age eight, witnessing uneven fights
daily between a brown
cichlid and his nemesis,
the fish tank's Darth Vader. The swordtailed tyrant
mantled in purest night

slowly starved his victim,
butting him from the sprinkled food.
Watching that fish weaken sickened me
into a wrathful god
who scooped and hurled the flailing devil
down our toilet bowl. By the next morning
the cichlid had recovered
enough to drive a smaller cichlid
from the food source: in the churning water
another terror reign was born,

another tyrant crowned.
What will you make or remake of this?
It might remind you how Sam Barrett found,
lodged in a fork of his
apple tree one May morning,
a water snake with gleaming fangs locked tight
around a still-quivering
robin snatched from a higher branch,
when he thought he had done with long nights
and winter was vanished quite.

THE SEA IS ALL ABOUT US

The carcasses of men and beasts
lie stately up upon its shelf, rotting ...
There is naked Nature ... wasting
no thought on man, nibbling at the cliffy shore.

Cape Cod   Henry D. Thoreau

The yapping pugs run *trembling* along the coast
            but you, as much as they, are *out*
of place and *shuddering at the vastness*
            of the sea's undoings, blue towers
collapsing into white foam ooze, sandspits
            clawed apart by easterlies
the sea unleashes like attack dogs. It's
            the bloodlust of a primeval,
thundering Old Testament sea that feasts
            on carcasses of men and beasts:

            your sea. Ours is all about
us, our unraveling of those Second Day
            gatherings of land and water,
felling forests that kept sea-storm away
            from habitat, scraping out
unreal real estate from the deep's holdings.
            There the lost beachfront Edens sit
on wooden stilts, stricken shorebirds caught
            by rising tides, each windowed wing
lying in state upon its shelf, rotting.

The sea's become a weapon in our hands.
           In salvoes, iridescent waves
of poisoned discharge fall on distant sands,
           infiltrating low-lying havens.
Toxic squads of upper-case letters
           (DDTs, PCBs) ride plastic
surfboards along the arteries of turtles,
           or drop from parents' beaks like candies
into the mouths of baby albatrosses.
           There naked Nature is wasting

           away, its rosy coral cheeks
colour-drained: reefs older than the oldest
           redwood forest drop live leafage,
the stripped limbs bleach to bone, the nests
           disperse. When our Fury has scaled
the food chain, from amoeba to seahorse
           to the last beached and songless whale,
who will listen for your plover's *faint peep*
           as it runs between the breakers,
no thought on man, nibbling at the cliffy shore?

RUINED FOUNDATIONS

Cato's half-obliterated cellar-hole
still remains, though known to few ...
concealed from the traveller by a fringe of pines ...
now filled with the smooth sumac.

Walden XIV   Henry D. Thoreau

Red-faced with passion when unconcerned
patriots let some innocent runaway
be strong-armed back to slavery,
you thought it a one-off sell-out – hadn't learned
the whole story, Harvard never
having revised its list of chronicles
past Caesar, Livy, or Ovid
to include those later transmigrations
that led to an unclassical
Cato's half-obliterated cellar-hole

beside the road to Concord. How you would
have raged if you had read the tale
of earlier betrayals, from Cato's sale
to his abandonment at Walden:
a pregnant wife and child, a bare cabin,
the family gifted with – in lieu
of trade or tools – his former master's surname.
Fragments of the tragic sequel
fifty years before your fierce rebuke
still remain, though known to few,

scattered among records kept by functionaries.
First, baby dies of *cancrum oris*,
a gangrenous disease that eats the face
and follows from the slow starvation
that grips them all; then dehydration wrings
the mother's neck, the father's lungs
collapse and sigh the germ to their sixteen-
year-old daughter, who succumbs
in months – the passing of Cato and his line
concealed from the traveller by a fringe of pines

owned by the man who bought the land from Cato's
former owner and who owned
the walnut trees Cato's hands had sown
to feed his children in a future
they never saw. You marvelled at that soil's
fertility, how *from dry sticks*
which had seemed to be dead, large buds unfolded,
tropical leaves greened and turned
deep red, the rough cellar under human wreckage
now filled with the smooth sumac.

FUGITIVES

I hear ... about trampling this law under foot.
Why, one need not go out of his way to do that.
This law rises not to the level of the head ...
its natural habitat is in the dirt.

"Slavery in Massachusetts"   Henry D. Thoreau

We hear much about walls and fugitives.
If our so-called fugitives could reach back over the wall
of time, to clasp hands with those who saved hunted lives
in your age, it might make them less fearful.
They need to be touched like Henry Williams, the runaway
slave you calmed and sheltered before you put him
on the train to Canada's safe haven.
Your friends petitioned Congress to repeal
the "Bloodhound Law," but not content with what
you heard about trampling this law under foot,

you acted, putting your own freedom at risk.
If you go walking now through poor Latino
suburbs near Atlanta or San Francisco,
you'll find no bloodhound eyes but tinted windows
of agents' purring cars, pretending sleep,
waiting to pounce on Maria at first light
as she goes out the door to the houses she cleans.
Savvy to your government's martinets,
you won't even think of approaching one to ask
why they must go out of their way to do that

when greater danger lodges in the mind
of their commander-in-chief; instead, you'll warn
Maria to stay home, counsel her friend
Ana to take Uber, not the car
whose broken headlight might see her to jail,
tell their neighbour Luis not to plead
his ticket at the courthouse, let them all
know others care. Pandering to blind
ignorance and enforced by blinkered hatred,
this law rises not to the level of the head,

its wall far baser than the racing hearts
determined to evade it. I can see you,
trusted and welcomed, in the two-room apartment
that fugitive Gabriela and Julio
share with their children, feeling more at home
beside the little altar of family snapshots
than you ever would behind the domed
white portico, under gilt-framed art
on loan to the chief chaser and lifter of skirts
whose natural habitat is in the dirt.

Any man who thought for himself ...
would naturally be a rebel ...
it was a legislating for
a few and not for all.

Journal, 21 August 1851   Henry D. Thoreau

You found the metaphor
in Mencius, an old world sage:
   seeds of a better life
need fresh soil to germinate.
   For you at first, that soil
meant home ground, a commonwealth
   rich in *freedom for all* –
not Canada, where *soldiery*
   and the priesthood held
any man who thought for himself

in check. Later, as rampant weeds
   of scam or slavery
choked off the most promising seeds,
   you felt you'd *lost a country:*
cast from Walden, you were dwelling
   wholly within hell.
So, amid 1960s turmoil
   when civilly disobedient
consciences once more were jailed,
   you would have been a rebel,

        but might, like me, have found
a new world, as if America
        and lands north had changed ground,
confirming thoughts that located
        the true America
in *that country where you are*
        at liberty. Mencius,
so change-conscious, might have opined
        that every lawmaker
was really legislating for

a new country, the ground ever
        shifting, early settlers
tilling land and then reverting
        into earth themselves,
winds resettling immigrant seeds
        that, taking hold in local
soil, ripen into flowering trees –
        though not in enclaves where
turf sits pristine behind high walls
        for the few but not for all.

This opening appeared as a ... light point on the horizon ...
on the edge of the lake, whose breadth a hair could have covered ...
We should not have suspected it to be visible
if the Indian had not drawn our attention to it.

The Maine Woods   Henry D. Thoreau

You ask if a greater miracle could occur
than *to look through each other's eyes for an instant.*
It takes most of your life, and a miracle-worker,
for you to see his deeper world within
your newer. The eyes are those of Joe Polis,
guide who becomes your teacher – *meteoulin*
in Abenaki, shaman of the Penobscot,
steering towards what you cannot spot at first
across wide water: the path through primeval forest.
This opening appears as a light point on the horizon,

alive with the same white-cored radiance
you'd held the night before when moosewood shards
lit up the inside of your cradled hand
as he lit up the inside of your head,
where you connected science's *phosphorescence*
with *Artoosoqu'*, the Abenaki word
for wetland-haunting will o' the wisps. They dance
among the moosewood branches, each tree crowned
with its circling spirits, kin to this wisp hovering
on the edge of the lake, whose breadth a hair could have
   covered,

but whose sign language *meteoulin* can read –
as his fingers spell braille etched by browsing deer
along the undergrowth, and his feet decipher
paths ancestors mapped on the forest floor.
Lost without a compass, you learn from him
how wind and sun created legible
directions in the woods: with southern limbs
drawn out by long light, stubby north ones trimmed
by winter blasts, trunks become compass needles
you would not have suspected to be visible.

There is so much about him you do not suspect,
living, as you still think you do, in a country
exceedingly new, unmapped and unexplored,
thinking his *Indian instinct* means he *does not carry
things in his head,* even as he tells you
every plant's medicinal properties.
He schools you in proper handling of a canoe
after naming you "Great Paddler" in Abenaki,
and though he knows it's not India he inhabits,
the "Indian" never draws your attention to it.

TIMBER

The Anglo-American can indeed cut down
this waving forest … but he cannot converse
with the spirit of the tree … read the poetry
and mythology which retire as he advances.

The Maine Woods   Henry D. Thoreau

The path you took from *what seemed brutish before*
to *I have much to learn* led through the forest
where Joe, your "Indian," became your teacher,
reading you spells from the trees' library –
to spirit tea from hemlock needles, charm
parchment from birch bark, call up pencil points
from black spruce twigs. Yet, even as you claimed
that nature *made a thousand revelations*
to "them" which are *secrets* to "us," your own
Anglo-Americans did indeed cut down

the forest and those who read its mysteries,
winged metal teeth chewing through rings
of woodland history, peoples for whom trees
were columned, green-roofed homes themselves falling
to tiny hidden blades breathed in – malaria,
smallpox, and a host of piercing fevers
that like a forest fire ate their heartwood.
The instruments then brought in, by surveyors
like you, could span, scan, scrutinize, and measure
the wasted forest, but could not converse

with sawn timber in the trees' dialects,
bark and magic trimmed from the living pith.
North of your border, clear-cutting spread unchecked
even through fields of seedlings, the young growth
uprooted, trucked to residential schools,
sheared and squared off in conformity
to alien rites and their unrelenting rules.
Some stubbornly resisted, some buckled,
some fled to scraps of forest, to seek peace
with the spirits of the trees, read the poetry

engraved in contraband language on their bark.
And some died. Air erased from each last breath
a poem, song, or story that had charmed
away the *rift* – as you saw it – a breach
opened by the *cleaver* of intellect
wielded by prejudice and mere appearance
between the human and the so-called lesser
life forms. The settler settled, dispossessed
of a wholeness woven into the dances
and mythologies riven by his advances.

I hear the sound of Heywood's brook ...
it seems to flow through my very bones ...
It allays some sandy heat in me ...
pure water falls into my heart.

Journal, 11 July 1851   Henry D. Thoreau

You're right – *this earth* is *but the lining of*
          your *inmost soul exposed* – because
that soul is lined with passages composed
          by earth's prolific hand, neither
some bard's wishful, far-fetched metaphors nor
          folklore from an uprooted folk,
but correspondences between inner
          and outer worlds. As, when surprise,
sickness or speed makes your pulse quicken,
          you hear the sound of Heywood's brook

surge through your arteries. The race of blood
          and swish of waters bear the same
signature: nature's undeflectable flood,
          an onrush sharing the momentum
that drives earth on its streambed through the stars.
          As when, at a hard white season's
swerve to the green, I stood on a hill near Creemore
          and heard happy weeping that spilled
from tiny rivulets the thaw had opened,
          it seemed to flow through my very bones.

The river is within us. And the bleak
        stretches of sand: for you, thirteen
years wide after your soulmate brother's death,
        until a scene of resurrection
unfolded in a freshly hatched moth's wings
        spreading, *revealing some new beauty*
every fifteen minutes, the wings' white fringe
        a scalloped foam like the lacework
spent waves knit on the beach of a calm sea.
        What allays some sandy heat in me

happened last summer at the Beaver River
        when spawning Chinook salmon scaled
the sharp-edged, high stone steps of a fish ladder,
        battering at each riser's wall,
falling back, gathering strength, hurling again
        until they reached the next rampart –
as my grandson Nicky that afternoon
        kept running at the tall hay bale
he finally scaled. When I think of that,
        pure water falls into my heart.

SEEING DOUBLES

It seemed as if I might next cast my line
upward into the air, as well as downward
into this element which was scarcely more dense.
Thus I caught two fishes as it were with one hook.

Walden IX   Henry D. Thoreau

Oh yes: two arms, two legs, two eyes, two ears –
that *dualism which nature loves* is clearly
written all over us. Rowing the Concord,
you read it in the water's seesawing colour
(sky blue to leafy green and back again)
and wrote it onto your boat, freshly painted
azure border cresting mossy hull
and white-winged sail riding finned beam below.
When you fished a surface flooded with sunshine
it seemed as if you might next cast your line

into that mirror and reel in a striped cloud
along with darker, weightier fish who lurked
far underneath; and when you and your brother –
introvert and extrovert who doubled for each other –
journeyed northwards to where the dawdling Concord
met the scurrying Merrimack, it appeared
you sailed some Arcadian stream where opposites
become one: so pondbound tadpoles refit
themselves as airborne frogs, or cedars spiral
upward into the air, while rooting downward,

or love makes *dreams* of those who love and are loved
mutually intelligible – that gift
you and your brother shared. After he died,
your body mimed his illness, as if you tried
to lose yourself in him. Coming to your senses
meant just that – eyes and ears would compensate
for being less than one soul. Seeing and hearing
more acutely would double the mirroring
power of nature: you would walk immersed
in an element which was scarcely more dense

than the air you breathed: imagination,
reaching out with all the senses to a nature
no *mere fragment of dead history*
but living poetry like the leaves of a tree –
a single, fish-boned leaf of your red oak
whose fins are watery bays on a first look,
but then suggest sharp-pointed rocky capes
until the eye sails round them and they deepen
to bays once more. Thus, in a double-take,
you catch two fishes as it were with one hook.

The fields are acquiring a greenish tinge ...
The element of water prevails ...
I hear the chattering of blackbirds ... smell the skunk ...
this circle of creatures completes the world.

Journal, 18 April 1852   Henry D. Thoreau

Not one to walk in a straight line
or follow rules and rulers, you prefer
     to view the spectrum of colours
as the year's great spinning wheel, winding
     its bright yarns onto earth's bobbin,
round sunflower faces mirroring
     that unblinking noon one in
the sky, apples already reddening;
     then, under blue mists of winter
the fields, acquiring a greenish tinge,

ripen to yellow when summer comes round again.
     For you, the Greeks' four elements
also step into the world's circle dance:
     earth, after drinking up spring rains,
casts away veils of white and pink, and lights
     into fresh rhythms, leaving trails
of green, which dry October days ignite
     to branching candle-fire, soon blown
to ash on chill air; after the last snowfalls
     the element of water prevails

once more, the river tossing in
its bed as dreams melt towards the sea. For you,
        the turn of seasons finds truest
footing in feet – two, four, or six returning
        annually: the nuthatch pauses
in its deft clamber around a ridged trunk
        to stutter *what-what-what-what* cause
brings it home; the northern flicker, cackling,
        picks at earth's sudden abundance;
you hear the chattering of blackbirds, smell the skunk,

watch the whirligig beetle dancing circles
        on the freshly thawed brook's surface,
and know from these signs that the heavens' dancers
        are bowing once more to their partners
in orbits like those you trace where honeybees
        abandon straight bee lines to twirl
the Os that in ecstatic semaphores
        spell nectar. For you, like the day's
skein of morning sun fully unfurled,
        this circle of creatures completes the world.

THE PATTERNS IN YOUR ROUNDS

I would fain keep a journal which should contain ...
impressions which I am most liable to forget ...
Which would have, in one sense the greatest remoteness –
in another the greatest nearness, to me.

Journal, after 10 January 1851   Henry D. Thoreau

A gamekeeper, you walk your rounds checking
          traps *set for facts*, no gun under
your arm, backpack with deep-storage pockets
          weighed down by a thinker's weapons –
lens, tape measure, pencil case, botanical guide,
          notebook – with room for shards of stone
or wood, leaf samples, lichens, nuts, and seeds.
          Not trusting memory's glowing sun
with objects grasped in moonlight, snow, or rain,
          you keep a journal which contains

the objects' imprints, vivid as fossil finds
          you've read about in Darwin, given
life beyond life, their tight-packed coaches riding
          into the future. Fossils save
the strong-boned outlines flesh once masked; so, purged
          of features time and water rot,
the patterns you preserve in your journal
          lie deep enough to *carry you back*
to more than that *day alone could show*, not
          just impressions you might forget

but the day within the day, the brother-self
        within the self – *as poetry*
discovers in a single May noon twelve
        months of *all one spring*, a Henry
in a henry – the sometime dweller in Walden
        now at home among the open
leaves of *Walden*. The backpack stuffed with Then
        spills out its wealth as present tense:
those finds you held with finger-gripping closeness
        have in one sense the greatest remoteness,

wood splinter having met its match through woodworm
        or match, seed having wakened from
its sleepy little life and been transformed
        to looming tree – itself unwoven
by storm – and pencil that sketched wood and seed
        whittled to sawdust. Still, though steeped
in centuries of their shared quiet, you speak
        the patterns of their lives through words
tight-packed in upper and lower case that keep
        their otherness in greatest nearness to me.

ROUNDS: THE CREEL

How many aboriginal ways
we ... should have learned from them. ... to know ...
weaving that creel ... was meditating
a small poem ... whose subject was spring.

Journal, 20 March 1858   Henry D. Thoreau

In the Pole Brook sluiceway you found
a homemade wonder just below
the glassy surface: deftly bound,
finger-thick tapered sticks of willow
set small end down in a circle –
a creel *very artfully* placed
on its long side, like a windsock
to catch gusts of eels. The wonder
ebbed to regret as your mind traced
how many aboriginal ways

slipped out of the ill-woven creel
of settler prejudice – not just
the knack or hang of wielded tools,
or inner compass to traverse
underbrush and undercurrents,
but the art of fitting into
a world we think fits in our hands.
If we had let them lead us through
the steps of their creative dance
we should have learned from them. You know

from journaling how we may mould
the patterns that contain us: so
Preston Singletary now rolls
the blowpipe with its molten globe
over the slab's marble waters
to frame a vessel his breathing
has filled, before his hands emboss
its sides with shapes from Tlingit lore.
Like glassblowing or like writing,
weaving that creel was meditating

on flow – of water or of ink,
of glass that hardens, or how sprays
of willow spring from stony trunks –
art's metaphors for history.
Glass breaks, brooks run dry, words grow dumb,
but history proves your gloom wrong
when it predicted *extinction*
for the creel's art. Turning, shaping,
Singletary's hands are singing
a small poem whose subject is spring.

III

Looking with Emily Carr

Before becoming known as a painter, Emily Carr
(1871–1945) achieved fame for her writing. In 1941,
she won the Governor General's Award for literature.
Although her reputation as artist has since largely
eclipsed her literary work, that work claimed equal
attention for most of her life, especially in her last
years when she found it less physically demanding than
painting. My glosas engage with Carr's passionate writing
about the natural environment, the well-being of non-
human animals, and the relationship between art and life,
always a matter of vital importance to her. Italicized
words and phrases within stanzas are direct quotations
from Carr's writings.

She took a big key and fitted it
into the padlock. The binding-chain fell away
from the pickets. I stepped with Mother
beyond the confines of our very fenced childhood.

Growing Pains, "Mother"   Emily Carr

Did you dream it, or was it real, that tale
          of picnicking among the white
blossoms? The aromatic field of lilies –
          their perfume's *power* to defeat
the challenge of *a black, tarred fence* – reeks
          pure myth, while your Mother figure
(*just right*, like the chair of Goldilocks)
          reaches into her reticule
and magics up a paradise, as if
          she took a big key and fitted it

          into the cloud-door, setting free
a sky *filled with sunshine*. You were Alice,
          squeezing through a *tiny, grassy*
opening, not to catch up with a rabbit
          but to escape the ogre Father
who confined the girls of the family
          in identical pinafores
of black and white. In Mother's snuggery,
          the ogre's *fadeless black* faded
into the shadows, the binding chains fell away,

and you made daisy chains while Mother stitched
        seams – *only a short while* before
she died. The lilies and daisies of that sheltered
        day also passed, but flowering
with them grew a perennial, brighter
        than the drab fabrics your Father
imposed on you, rooted in the art that brought
        loving attachment to the swatches
of daisies your small, sunlit hands gathered
        from the thicket steeped in your Mother's

        devoted magic. The same vision
that saw or dreamt how flowers might transform
        fetters into pinwheeled festoons
would conjure up the Tall of fallen totems,
        roam animal otherness deep
in eyes whose *whites* were *brown* and, by freehand,
        sound churning depths in forests that seemed
grounded. Climbing astride a white horse dappled
        with myth and magic, you rode it
beyond the confines of your fenced childhood.

TREE TALK

Enter into the life of the trees.
Know your relationship and understand
their language, unspoken, unwritten talk.
Answer back to them ... soul words, earth words.

Journal, 12 November 1932   Emily Carr

Where can I find your living soul?
Not photographs, where clothes and pose
conceal. Not canvases, their oil
darkened and cracked. One late touch holds
a clue: the same red-brown pigment
kindling your *Forest* trunks imbues
your *Self-Portrait*, a whispered hint
of kinship among the *free and wild*.
To draw near me, the portrait says,
enter into the life of the trees.

As you did, half-orphan refuged under
the Garry oak whose lap of roots
held you *in their quiet fastness*,
and whose fingers – after winter
had thinned them down to whitened bone –
fluttered to life and overflowed
each spring with catkin rings: no words,
but a leaf-lisp of continued
lullaby, as if the woods
knew your relationship and understood

your longing for a foster home
as far beneath human language
as roots reach beneath *the turmoil
of undergrowth* and its tangled
syntax in search of sister-roots,
mainstays in a social network
whose conversations your art grew
to enter into, the mute, fluent
handle of your brush nodding back
their language: unspoken, unwritten talk.

The oak and its companion trees
furnished a home for you and for
a sisterhood of wild *creatures*:
the monkey curled up in her cedar –
cuddled into its very heart –
inhaled its peace, as you breathed in
from the pines' *honourable straightness
perfume* in response to your caress,
and when winds talked through leaves, the birds
answered back to them soul words, earth words.

EPPING FOREST

No turmoil of undergrowth swirling round
the boles ... no fallen branches ...
no awed hush, no vast echoes ...
perfect ... but not for ... Canadians

Growing Pains, "Martyn"   Emily Carr

Your motherland turned out
to be a fatherland – rulebound,
life's quirky curves pruned straight-edged
          as his garden hedges.
"You must not walk upon the grass,"
          the Kew caretaker frowns;
yet when you abandon their lawns
          and search for wilderness
          in their "forest," you find
no turmoil of undergrowth swirling round

rotten stumps, no brambles blocking
          footfalls, reaching to scratch
unwary legs, no spooked raccoons
          skittering out of reach,
          but an embalmed vista,
trunks trim as a vault's stone arches.
Where are the real forest's downed trees,
          those overturned canoes
beached inland when storms unanchored
          the boles – fallen branches

                    left adrift like paddles?
Epping Forest might have been
hung in the National Gallery,
                    its leaves all *smiling* green,
a landscape "done" in every sense,
                    framed by straight paved roads
                    and *a mile-high iron fence.*
Your cupped ear catches harmony
          fit for a child's dollhouse:
no awed hush, no vast echoes

slip through the incessant *sweetness*
                    of robins who sound caged.
Sprinkled with filtered sun, you miss
                    the *downpour of cackling*
honks scattering like hailstones while
                    wild geese *sail above man's*
reach, their flock's prow arrowing
                    through cloud. Some might find this
forest's mummified elegance
                    perfect, but not this Canadian.

TWO RUINS

The rank smell of nettles and rotten wood,
the lush greens of the rank sea grass ...
and the great dense forest behind
full of unseen things and great silence.

Journal, 1 February 1931   Emily Carr

The two might have been one, the same village
            painted onto different backdrops.
            Part the grass curtains, and reveal
cedar saplings poking through collapsed
roof panels, long-necked mushroom nestlings craning
            from corner posts, crossbeams hooded
            with moss. Your palette thins to green
and grey. You sense the same unpaintables
            in both places – the moaning wind,
the rank smell of nettles and rotting wood,

salt riding the damp air from waves to tongue –
            and as your brushwork labours so
            that eyes may grasp the sense of touch,
art wakens to differences between the two
ruins: the *mushroom town* of Skagway, home
            to none, mere loam for the rootless
            boot to jump from, and the longtime-
tended soil of Skedans, an anchorage
even when unpeopled, still graced by
            the lush greens of the rank sea grass,

sun-cracks in the grey totems adding fresh
        wisdom-wrinkles to the faces,
        and *bones* – not the scatter of bleached
animal bones along the Skagway wayside
broken under burdens of man's greed,
        but cherished elders' bones aligned
        in coffins perched above the beach
on mortuary poles, keeping watch
over the sea's incursions on the shoreline
        and the great dense forest behind

the row of longhouses. You went to school
        at Skedans, learning from the dead
        who would not stay dead – *so full*
of vitality was this place where *every seed*
germinated and burst into life, even
        the seeds of art. You learned to sense
        things hidden, *felt rather than seen,*
and built, for feelings beneath sound or smell,
        homes in house paint, on canvases
full of unseen things and great silence.

KITWANCOOL SHANTY

The floor was of earth and the walls were of cedar ...
they had breathed themselves into it
as a bird, with its head under its wing,
breathes itself into its own cosiness.

Klee Wyck, "Kitwancool"   Emily Carr

The local seat of government,
home to the chief and her husband,
suited you better than the ornate
massive new pile of Romanesque
stone in Victoria, which housed
the wind in tomb-like white marble.
From their shanty – a nest *made round*
them – logs in the firepit sent
warm breath into the chill night air.
The floor was of earth and the walls were of cedar,

as in the forest, and a real
woman (not the Legislature's
hewn or painted allegories)
ate and slept there with her consort.
No hills were levelled, no quarries
rifled in the little lean-to's
making, no more than a turtle
plunders the beach to roof itself.
The couple fit their space as if
they had breathed themselves into it,

84

the way a woman in childbirth
breathing new life into the world
bodies herself as a mother.
Outside, a totem infant curled
tightly within the wooden walls
of mother's arms, her embracing
hands enlarged to signify them *full
of tenderness*, her infant's face
wide-eyed behind closed lids, sleeping
as a bird with its head under its wing

sleeps, but *wrapped up under her heart,
the cosiest.* One with the life
surrounding them, one with its art,
the Kitwancool husband and wife
lay down at night beside the fire
on cedar plank and fur mattress.
Above the shanty, ravens shared
the smoke hole's warmth. Around their nest,
blanketed with mist, the forest
breathed itself into its own cosiness.

UNSHELTERED

Solitude, no shelter, exposed
to all the 'winds' like a lone old tree
with no others round
to strengthen it against the buffets.

Journal, 6 April 1934   Emily Carr

Fast forward on your part, rewind
            on mine, and we will meet
under the unumbrella'd sign
            at Unsheltered: you'll leap
from new growth forest to the heath
            of middle age; I'll coast
back down from higher years to deeps
            of childhood angst. Hounded
round the clock by boarders, you've lost
            solitude: no shelter, exposed

            at the easel *as if*
in my bathtub. Soon, need has torn
            the paintbrush from your grip
and in its place a wooden spoon
            stirs porridge, and a scuttle
feeds black breakfasts to a *greedy*
            hellmouth or uncovers
whitened walks. And flings gifts of an
            artist-turned-landlady
to all the winds like a lone old tree's

leaves in autumn. *The weight of the house*
        crushed your soul, but the lack
of one left mine, at six, confused:
        if Mommy did come back
where would that be? "Aunt" Marian's
        cold water flat downtown
had one daybed – for me. The Orbans'
        two boys shared an alcove.
Daddy slept at work on a couch
        with no others round.

        My mother came back to
our old apartment, my wonder
        couched in that "F" word you
bluntly embraced. "Mommy, you were
        Fatter." You and I would
shelter further under art's roof:
        once it has taken hold,
its embrace *will not give up,*
        feeding the soul with life
to strengthen it against the buffets.

Nodding and laughing ... he sawed ... as if aeons
of time were before him ... Life had sweetened
the old man. He was luscious with time
like the end berries of the strawberry season.

Klee Wyck, "Ucluelet"   Emily Carr

You came upon him in *this place belonging*
neither to sea nor to land, a strip of sand
too awash with salt for roots to grip,
too rooted on its ledge for tides to sunder:
old man sawing and smiling; his instrument's teeth,
as they lilted through a wind-toppled shore pine,
filled out songs from his nearly toothless mouth.
Then you and he conversed, in hand motions,
of ancient things – sun, land, sea – until again
nodding and laughing he sawed, as if aeons

were being sawn, each sweep cutting across
another growth-ring year. My father, who
had spent his working years as a specialist
in time-and-motion study, later grew
careless of both, cutting back on motion
and giving up on time, at twilight reaching
a place near that old man's, a windy beachhead
setting off bounded forest from boundless ocean.
Punch clock, stopwatch, the tick-tock threatenings
of time were behind him. Life had shortened

to a narrow strip of sand set in pure present.
Unlike the old singer logging his years,
my father – room number pinned to shirtfront
in the nursing home, shuffling in slippers –
dwindled, as if the old times he stood upon
had eroded out from underneath him,
leaving him far shorter than the son
who, stooping, ambled alongside. But unbent
under a *shock* of *grizzled* hair, still strong-limbed,
your old man was luscious with a time

that coasted on waves, not one spun by wheels.
A life inhaling sea-mist, also waveborne,
mingled preserving brine with the salt that flowed
through the tributaries of his body.
Songs from his lips found stronger counterpoint
in humming cedar branches than in the measures
thrown off by his saw: he had ripened
into deeper tones, like last year's bronzed
leaves overwintering on oak trees, or
like the end berries of the strawberry season.

TOTEMS

Bird eyes were humanly shaped and deep-set ...
overhung by a heavy eyebrow painted black ...
huge square ears ... on ... top of the head ...
You felt the lift and sweep of the carved wings.

The Heart of a Peacock, "Indian Bird Carving"   Emily Carr

"Nature, Mr Allnut, is what we are
          put in this world to rise above,"
says Hepburn's Rose to Bogart's Charlie,
          nutshelling what you never believed.
Nature is what we are, you say, inter-
          woven threads in the same carpet,
like those you watch the Haida women weave
          from old clothes and cedar fibre.
So, on a Skidegate housefront totem,
          bird eyes are humanly shaped and deep-set,

          irises shining from the rimmed
oblong of white that looks out from your mirror –
          these interminglings no mere whim
but the skilled art of a Haida carver
          who *knew his bird,* and also knew
more than your sisters when they took
          straightlaced Rose's role and cast you
as uncouth Charlie, scorning your attic mural
          because you'd pictured Eagle's beak
overhung by a heavy eyebrow painted black.

Sleeping under that mural brought *strong dreams:*
          trees *burning green in every leaf,*
root-talons sunk into the ground, brooded
          over by branches, spread plumage.
Like the totems' *deep symbolical carving,*
          this dream-steeped brushwork depicted
nature's meshwork, *every scrap of it vital –*
          so, painting a weathered beaver,
your hand followed the sculptor's, which had fixed
          huge square ears on top of the head

          to capture *attributes*, not likeness,
treating ears as portals, doorways of sound
          that, unseen, takes the air and glides
from the seashore into the body's house.
          Unseen too: features of soul
that wing the image with life, *weight, power, being.*
          When homaging a raven pole,
you cannot lay the brush down, will not close
          your eyes, until through the painting
you feel the lift and sweep of the carved wings.

BIRD HOUSE

Lay the foundations ... on the croaks of the crows and the jays ...
Fill it with thrush songs and blackbirds ... wrap
the great white owl's silent wings round it
and let the nightingale sing it to sleep.

Journal, 29 May 1934   Emily Carr

       Ordinary houses wrong us –
strand us in the emptiness of fallen
       Skedans corner posts, or drown us
in overfulness like the boarding house
       you landladyed – but the Haida
lived in their totems, carved out space inside
       the creature that was their ideal:
eyes their windows, heart their hearth, throat their song.
       To build your ideal house, you lay
the foundations on the croaks of the crows and the jays,

sounds down to earth as any avian
       can be – birds making no pretense
to permanence, being there then gone
       on air their calls fill with emptiness.
From the black cellar of the crow's feathers
       rises a flight of creaking steps,
flooded with blue light when the jay's cry squeaks
       a trap door open to the main
floor. Once the avocet gives a *sweep, sweep,*
       fill it with thrush songs and blackbird rap,

                sink into the Victorian
upholstery of a mourning dove's coverts,
                and spend an hour deciphering
the calligraphy of redwings' crossword-
                puzzled eggshells. Where do we live
if not as figures within the living ground
                of other high flyers? We weave
a scavenger house of comings and goings,
                and at the evening's end we wind
the great white owl's silent wings round it

and sleep; and if our rest is broken by
                a Cooper's hawk's harsh treetop scorn
or a common loon's waterborne cry,
                we'll listen for the miniature
boat horn of the nuthatch Thoreau says
                is "giving vent" in that *peep-peep*
"to the spring within it." We will book passage
                on its houseboat-lullaby
for shores covered with sweet blossoming dreams,
                and let the whippoorwill sing us back to sleep.

His head ... sparkling ... rested on my shoulder ...
I sensed the loneliness of this creature ...
no kith, no kin: his looking-glass self
the only mate he had ever known.

The Heart of a Peacock [title-piece]   Emily Carr

As out of place as you, as cooped
within Victoria, he leaped
the public garden fence, and after
brief dalliance with a cherry tree
all frily spring plumage, he spied
the mirror of your folded-back
dormer window. Preening, he played
Narcissus in it; art-occupied,
you missed his bolder steps, until
his head, sparkling, rested on your shoulder.

While you sat drawing at your easel
honouring April with pastels,
he seemed – you caught the irony –
to draw glory out of the tree
he used as backdrop for the spread
splendour of his tail, but then – reaching
his long neck out – cradled his head
on you in seeming sympathy.
Drawn from a focus on his own features,
he sensed the loneliness of this creature

who flourished a palette as bright
as his, and like him took to flight
when crowd-threatened, but who thirsted
for *a really kindred spirit*
to *share* the *spring green* and the waves'
steely blue – those peacock hues, held
shimmering in the crown he gave
into your care. In you he met
another solitary self,
no kith, no kin: his looking-glass half

come through the looking-glass to caress
his pillowed head. You learned his cry,
the *long-drawn tang of bitterness*
that voiced what you had held inside
since childhood. When the zookeepers
caged him to curtail his roaming,
his head sagged forward, wings drooped.
All the glint went off his feathers,
the painted eyes blurred in mourning
the only mate he had ever known.

ANIMAL TALK

Determination to fulfill
their span of life and ... perpetuate their kind:
these are a creature's full expression.
He does not have to grin, he expresses himself all over.

This and That, "Grinning"   Emily Carr

They are the living pop-up books we read
          in the world's outdoor library.
Some, like hummingbirds, lend themselves to speed
          reading; some, more deliberate,
school us in patience, as when a burdened
          donkey trudges up mountain trails
or dozens of generations of termites
          build highrise mounds. You deciphered
how the quick back-and-forth of swallows spelled
          determination to fill full

          their nestlings' craning mouths, and we
construe their favoured range most vividly
          from the sea-green of neck feathers
or a song's liquid chortle, rather than from
          their *thalassina* species-tag.
They are avid readers too, alert to sign
          and nuance – though we take a lack
of words for lack of language and believe
          their lot is dumbly to unwind
their span of life and perpetuate their kind.

The smallest sparrow spends her waking hours
        scanning invisible currents,
perusing flows and eddies to allow for
        the minute muscular adjustments
that maintain her balance and momentum,
        while your large sheepdog focuses
on the orthography of line and furrow
        passing moods write across your brow,
responding in the kinetic esperanto
        that is a creature's full expression:

        bob of head, swish of tail, as limbs
tremble and *dance and leap with joy,* or fold
        in on themselves in sympathy.
Non-human animals read and write with their whole
        beings. Love-letters fill the ear
around branches where the male swallow hovers;
        below, a cat-chased squirrel's fear
ripples through a body where thoughts of climbing,
        muscle, and bone are interleaved.
He does not need a pen, he expresses himself all over.

CALLINGS

Part of an artist's queer equipment ...
Every object must be felt, smelt, tasted,
pulled to pieces before
her curiosity was satisfied.

The Heart of a Peacock, "Woo's Calls"   Emily Carr

She named herself that first night, wailing out
        "Woo, woo" until exhaustion shut
eyes and then mouth. The power of her naming –
        Woo she remained for life – proclaimed
she'd never meekly be your monkey or
        anyone else's, and hinted
that giving voice to loneliness might *comfort*
        the little beast within the heart.
After the night of her calling, Woo wasn't
        part of an artist's queer equipment,

        but was herself an artist, *surprised*
at her own hands, looking at them intently,
        proud of the grasp that terrorized
your mocking parrot when Woo reached to wrench
        tailfeathers for the collages
flung, smeared, or dribbled as she disastered
        your dresser, ripping out pages,
drinking the bottle of ink, chewing the pen,
        none of her senses wasted as
every object must be felt, smelt, tasted,

not merely seen and heard. Mystic as well,
 she moved beyond the senses towards
a grinning *other monkey* her hands felt for
 behind the mirror – unrewarded,
never closing on something huggable.
 Those hands, better at exploring
than securing, suited legs unable
 to abide restraint, the flannel
outfit you tailored for her torn apart,
 pulled to pieces before

 she'd worn it ten minutes: like her
keeper, Woo treasured freedom over warmth.
 Looking into her irises,
clear and golden, you must have seen yourself
 imaged in the fierce purity
of the uncompromising search that guided
 her agile hand: you would surely
have felt you'd missed your calling if ever,
 right up to the hour you died,
your curiosity was satisfied.

CONNECTIONS

A tiny, dainty, swaying bell
silently ringing with the slightest breeze.
The organs on each side of your head
don't register the sound but the soul does.

Journal, 3 November 1938   Emily Carr

When the wind blows, spillage of music pours
          from the fuchsia's upside-down
cups, and ears more finely tuned than ours
          drink it. Our eyes miss subtle tones
of UV light guiding, like flaming beacons,
          hummingbirds to the cinquefoil's
sweet core. The odour-trails from plankton,
          grazed by petrels foraging
the waves, escape our nostrils. Clapperless,
          a tiny, dainty, swaying bell

          tolls out our species' failure to
connect with all the wonders of the air.
          We stand under a waterfall,
possessed of speech yet senseless as a stone
          to swirling eddies that caress
the fur or feathers of our wordless kin.
          We forge sun-bright, cloud-climbing wings
and roar aloft, but the same air we think
          we rule serves them invisibly,
silently bringing, on the slightest breeze,

delicacies for tongue or tympanum.
Water and earth, like air, unfurl
sensory welcome mats for them – salmon
follow the streams' olfactory
GPS back to spawning grounds, while sand-
pipers' probing bill tips are cued
by seismic vibes towards tunnelling shore crabs.
Elephants stay online with fellow
elephants through their paired networks: besides
the organs on each side of their heads –

those floppy grey satellite dishes –
their grounded legs pick up low frequency
signals from one another as
they stamp distant paths. And you, Emily,
in that van you've named The Elephant,
what server lets you hear what you call "screamers,"
chords in the tree's very heart,
broken when it was felled, back *years and years*
and now haunting the stump? Your ears
don't register the sound but your soul does.

She seemed to be part of the tree itself,
as if she had grown there at its heart ...
the voice of the tree ... might have burst
from that great round cavity ... her mouth.

Klee Wyck, "D'Sonoqua"   Emily Carr

Your starched white neighbours might have thought –
had they the wherewithal to think –
D'Sonoqua was your self-portrait:
wild woman, hands grimed, hair unkempt,
more at home with forest creatures
than with her own kin. Her carver
had chiselled minimal features,
her trunk the red cedar's trunk,
and with legs hidden in rank turf
she seemed to be part of the tree itself,

finger-stubs leafless twigs, round mouth
a knothole: dendro-woman taken
mid-transformation. Eyes uncouth
black blanks – not your *landlady* look
of burnout, but the dark of deep space,
outer or inner, creative
hub, whirling vortex more than place.
Less a work of human making
than the forest's own organic art,
as if she had grown there at its heart.

She was all circles, from the round
ears that *stuck out to catch all sounds,*
down through the *column* of her neck,
along arms *spliced and socketed*
into the trunk and flung out, in
a wide arc, as if she embraced
the wheeling waves her torso faced
in maternal or priestly greeting,
and when wind rolled through the forest,
the voice of the tree might have blessed

the salt air and the circling clouds,
and you, brought to your knees by that
apparition of D'Sonoqua
on a slippery disused footpath.
Her image lived like an icon
hidden at the back of your thoughts
for twenty years until, marking
a new turn for your brush, the breath
of inspiration spiralled out
from that great round cavity, her mouth.

The poor, muddled brain fretting
over captivity has been released for spells …
No bars of asylums or jails or poverty …
can arrest the flight of our imaginings.

Journal, 31 March 1934   Emily Carr

When you visit Harold *with his white face*
          and damaged forehead, do the eyes
of your soul twitch in horror at the place?
          Iron grated doors, barred windows,
stairway a cage – moony imagination's
          dark side not letting you forget
your nightmare decade of incarceration
          as the head inmate of Hill House,
its maze of furnished rooms a setting for
          the poor, muddled brain fretting

          among locked opportunities,
brief jailbreaks sketching northern trees for paintings
          aborted by your poverty.
Harold's landlady-like chores – polishing
          his asylum's brass spittoons,
setting places at the long refectory tables –
          have stolen hours he might have spent
perfecting his art, but now, kneeling at
          the chair he's made a desk, he tells you
his captivity's over: he's been released. He spells

out freedom in the transcript of his life,
             quite good in spots and wild romance
in others, happenings spread out map-like,
             with all the rivers and hills showing,
pencil and paper bringing him – as you –
             strong easement for perplexity.
Each page, like a paper plane, sails through
             the cage and over the laughter
of his inmates or yours. Like earth's *green sea,*
             no bars of asylums or jails or poverty

             can stop a story tree's break-out
and climb-up to the light, one tree seeding
             the next, as you two talk about
villages we both know and creatures
             we both love. You're like that totem
where Bear embraces a human youngster
             above the niche where Human embraces
a cub. Most of the totem's crowning eagle
             has fallen, but no lack of wings
can arrest the flight of your imaginings.

CLUMSY LIFE AGAIN

Just put a peach in my pocket and sat on it,
left the fish I'd prepared at home,
knocked the pickle bottle across my glasses
and broke them, and broke the van window.

Journal, 5 September 1934   Emily Carr

Chaos everywhere! You wave
the iodine bottle to bring home a point
          and drench Mrs McMuir, whose oven
makes toast of your toast. Unchained, Woo paints
          the basement floor in linseed oil
and egg, her lips with blueing, your garden bonnet
          with liquid tar – the sticky puddles
of black and yellow a worse mess than when
          the dogs broke into the meat pot,
you put a peach in your pocket and sat on it,

and the cracked kettle turned your Majestic stove
          into a thermal spring. Still, you'd
rather stick to your credo (*You've got to love*
          things right through) than spurn as "stupid"
the awkward "confusion" of "clumsy Life,"
          cast off as "waste" by Henry James,
your fellow storyteller, in his "sublime
          economy of art." More grounded,
you practise a kitchen economy,
          like it fresh, carry it right home

and use it, think *even sketches*
are canned food. You seek an art rooted in earth,
            where *it bursts forth like a struck match*
in perfect leaves the trees craft without theory,
            a squirrel's unerring jeté,
a gull's tucked wave-dive, or the flash from a bass's
            seamless hood of silver lamé
so you regarded it as a blessing
            when, while camping, clumsiness
knocked the pickle bottle across your glasses,

depriving you of print and forcing you
            to focus on the tints under
your nose – scarlet of rose hips, brown russet
            of bracken, parched grass hardened
into silver wire ripples – miles away
            from pallid pinks and bleached yellows,
the *tinkling landscapes* kept like hothouse flowers
            behind glass in the Crystal Gardens,
until the loved things in your solo show
            bloomed, and broke open those vain windows.

SKIDEGATE SANDS

Sea, sky, and beach ... smoothed into one ...
Of that pink spread silence even
I had become part, belonging
as much to sky as to earth.

Klee Wyck, "Salt Water"   Emily Carr

Your paintings won't sit still: silver-
white shifts ground downward to yellow-
brown, darks lighten, cheap manila
paper takes on a deep golden
glow, everything ever on the
go: *continuous movement* un-
daunting to you who caught the sun's
quick brushwork at Skidegate fill-
ing dawn's canvas for an instant,
sea, sky, and beach smoothed into one

blanketing pink a twinkling's re-
touching turned to pentimento
under bands of glossy peacock,
cyan, and the sand's flat tawny
beige. And didn't you become one
with that movement at evening when
you lay down on the river stones
letting *the water ripple o-*
ver: from your *sixty-year-old skin*
pink whispered through silence even-

ly as the stream *and there was life*
in the soft blackness of the night.
The trees breathed in your breath, and leaf-
chatter, in counterpoint, fluted
into your ears – as on those pole-
sentries at Skidegate lining
the path, where all the figures told
a shared tale of transformation:
finned, winged, or footed, each single
"I" had become a part, belonging

to the multifoliate tree
of life, whose roots and branches shift
places with one another, freed
from finish into grip and lift.
So, on your *Shoreline*, cliffs tremble
and break like waves below cloudbursts,
while at water's edge the scumbled
sand bears streaked clouds like a river,
each brushstroke shimmer giving birth
as much to sky as to earth.

"Callings": Chiang-ning, present day Nanjing, is the southeast China city near which Wang An-shih lived. Ch'an is a tradition of Mahayana Buddhism that flourished in China before and during his lifetime.

"Transport": Peachblossom Land was a legendary ideal village caught in a time-warp.

"Butterflies": The *Book of Changes*, or *I Ching*, is an ancient Chinese divination text, dating back as far as the tenth century BCE. Chunyu Fen is the main character in Li Kung-tso's ninth-century story, *The Governor of the Southern Tributary State*. Chuang Tzu was a fourth century BCE Taoist philosopher. *The Ancient Mirror* is a seventh-century story by Wang Tu. The *guqin* is a plucked, stringed instrument associated with ancient Chinese scholars and literati.

"The Voicing Room": Often made of mother-of-pearl, *hui* are inlaid dots on the *guqin*. The Pearl is a river system in southern China. The wood of the wutong tree is used for the soundboards of several Chinese instruments because of its superior acoustic properties.

"Ruins 2": The Narrows is the strait that runs between Brooklyn and Staten Island. Gowanus is the name of a canal emptying into the Narrows and of the Brooklyn neighbourhood bordering on the canal.

"Anchorage": The poet Li Po, or Li Bai, is famously said to have drowned while trying to embrace the moon's image in a river. Associated with regeneration, Tai Mountain is a sacred mountain in Shandong province.

"Islands 2": Threatened with devastating erosion from climate change, Lennox Island is a Mi'kmaq Nation off the coast of Prince Edward Island. Like Prince Edward Island's Ladyslipper flower, the Yangtze dolphin is virtually extinct as a result of environmental mismanagement.

"Nothing but the Wild Rain": Po Chü-i was a Tang Dynasty poet who, in a famous poem, wrote about rescuing a starving wild goose in desperate times.

"Double Exposure": *Riverbank* is a landscape scroll painted by Dong Yuan, active from the 930s to the 960s.

"The Country of Your Past": Xie Ling-yün, Meng Haoran, Du Fu, and Po-Chü-i were some of Wang An-shih's poetic precursors.

"Scope": Ralph Waldo Emerson, Thoreau's sometime mentor, wrote in "Nature" (1836), "I become a transparent eyeball; I am nothing; I see all; the currents of the Universal Being circulate through me; I am part or particle of God."

"The Harp": The Deep Cut was the railway embankment at Walden, along which telegraph wires were strung in 1852. Thoreau loved the music made by the wind as it passed through the wires.

"Combatants": Thoreau describes the battle of the ants in *Walden* XII.

"Ruined Foundations": For the full story of Cato Ingraham, see Elise Lemire, *Black Walden: Slavery and Its Aftermath in Walden* (Philadelphia: University of Pennsylvania Press, 2009), 122–7.

"A Deeper World": For a discussion of Thoreau's relationship with Joe Polis and its impact on him, see chapter 10 of Laura Dassow Walls's *Henry David Thoreau: A Life* (Chicago: University of Chicago Press, 2017).

"Rounds: The Creel": The art of the Tlinkit glassblower Preston Singletary is comprehensively discussed in *Preston Singletary: Echoes, Fire and Shadow* (Tacoma and Seattle: Museum of Glass and University of Washington Press, 2009).

"Epping Forest": While studying art in London, Carr visited Epping Forest in September 1900.

"Kitwancool Shanty": Carr painted "Mrs. Douse, Chieftainess of Kitwancool," in 1928 after a visit to the village.

"Totems": Rose and Charlie are the main characters in John Huston's film, *The African Queen* (1951).

"Callings": Carr looked after the Javanese monkey Woo from 1921 until 1937, when declining health made it impossible for her to tend to the needs of her animals.

"Forest Spirit": Carr encountered images of D'Sonoqua in several villages. The description in *Klee Wyck* arose from her visit to the Kwakiutl village of Quattiche in 1930.

"Mirror 2": Carr befriended Harold Cook, an inmate at the Provincial Mental Home near Victoria, and made frequent trips to see him. They often talked about Indigenous villages they both knew, and about animals. She provided him with the materials to write the story of his life.

ACKNOWLEDGMENTS

Earlier versions of these poems, sometimes with different titles, appeared in *Audeamus*, *The Fiddlehead*, and *Vallum*, and in the chapbook, *Conversing with Wang An-shih: A Sequence of Glosas* (Junction Books, 2018). I want to thank the editors for their encouragement, and especially Carleton Wilson for his inspiring book design and his long friendship.

Poems in this book's first section were inspired by David Hinton's luminous translations in *The Late Poems of Wang An-shih* (New Directions, 2015). His versions of Chinese writers and his reflections on literature and landscape – like those of my friends Roo Borson and Kim Maltman – have long enriched my thinking and writing. With characteristic generosity, he has given me permission to use his translations of Wang's quatrains as the source-poems for my glosas.

Other friends have also helped to shape the course of individual poems and the direction of the book as a whole. For years Zhou Yan and the late Bruce Nagle shared their knowledge of Chinese philosophical and literary traditions. Bruce also suggested fruitful approaches to Thoreau's writings, as did John Barton to Carr's. Once again, the members of the Vic group have generously brought their critical and kind attention to my writing; this time, I owe a particularly large debt to Allan Briesmaster, Sue Chenette, Carla Hartsfield, Maureen Hynes, K.D. Miller, and Leif Vaage. More broadly, Don McKay and Maureen Scott Harris have in their writings and their conversations contributed much to my understanding of the relationships between humanity and the environment we share with other life forms. At McGill-Queen's, Allan Hepburn has been a resourceful and enthusiastic editor and has rescued me from unwieldy constructions. Lastly, my wife Julie did not live long enough to see this book in print, but during her life sustained the richest of all conversations with me and with my writing.